The Lion of Damascus:
The Life of Hafez al-Assad

CW01501914

Written by:
Ovidijus Gelzinis

Table of Contents

Chapter 1 – The Son

In the mountainous area of Qurdaha, which is now a town in Western Syria, Assad's grandfather, Sulayman al-Wahhish was known as a strong man and was admired in his village. He exercised great power. If there were quarrels that could not be solved, a third man – *qadi* would be appointed as a judge. It was a role that Sulayman regularly played. His son 'Ali Sulayman inherited many qualities of his father. Like his father, 'Ali Sulayman was widely respected and was seen in the village as a strong and brave person. He continued the family tradition of resolving quarrels. He would live a long life, born in 1875, witnessing Ottoman Turkish rule, then the French and living until 1963, the year when the Ba'ath party came to power, which brought his son, Hafez to power. He was married twice, first to Sa'da who bore him five children, then Na'isa who bore him six, the fourth being Hafez and for 'Ali, his ninth child.

1927 was an important year for the al-Wahhish. Because of the esteem that 'Ali's family had earned over the two generations, the family's name was changed from Wahhish, which meant *savage* to Assad, which meant *lion*. Three years later, in 1930, Hafez Al-Assad was born in a two-room flat-roofed house in Qurdaha. The town at that time consisted of a hundred or so mud and stone houses at the end of the muddy track. It had no mosque, nor church and no shop, no café, no paved road and there was no village centre. *Mazar* was a place where people regularly gathered. It was a white-domed shrine of local saints, which was the mountains only type of religious architecture.

Hafez lived with a large family. Not only he was the ninth child of his father's family, just down the road lived his Uncle 'Aziz Sulayman and his seven cousins. The eldest cousin Manira was just a month younger than himself. He also had three aunts, who had married in into families in the nearby villages, which provided the chance for visits to yet more cousins. His Aunt Sa'da was to be particularly important to him because she married Ahmad Makhluf of the village of Bustan al-Basha, who was a close relative of the girl that would become his wife. His father's first five children, rather than being more like brothers and sisters, acted like uncles and aunts to Hafez, and their children, nephews to Hafez added fresh faces every year to the expanding family.

But the centre of Hafez's life, the Patriarch of the family was his father, 'Ali Sulayman. He was already fifty-five when Assad was born. In traditional Arab fashion, he was not only loved by his children, but also respected and obeyed. The boys would kiss his hand in the mornings and would not sit down in his presence. His mother, Na'isa, who was much younger than her husband, was a strong-minded woman in her own right and increasingly became the dominant parent. She had a particular influence over her two youngest sons – Jamil born in 1933 and Ri'fat born in 1937. Ri'fat who was a mischievous and lively child was her favourite.

Hafez spent his early years mostly outdoors. He perched on a donkey on the way to the fields. He helped with the watering of the crops or with the gathering of the fruit or maybe just scampering about in the mountains with friends. For many of those children, education did not feature in their lives. Illiteracy was mostly universal in the mountain settlements. Even in 1943-1944, less than a quarter of all Syrian children attended school. But Hafez would be luckier than the others. His father, 'Ali had respect for book learning. Although radio was not available, he was able to subscribe to a newspaper, which arrived several days late and was the only man in his village who followed the flow of the Second World War, pin-pointing battles on a wall-map in the room where Hafez slept as a boy. 'Ali was determined to educate his sons. His first eight children had no schooling to speak of because none had been available in the mountains. The Turkish authorities discouraged even basic learning and oppressed the village leaders who secretly tried to teach boys under a tree. But it was different with the more liberal French, who took control over the territory of Syria after the surrender of the Ottoman Empire at the end of the First World War. During the French rule, open-air classes were common, and it was in one of these classes that Hafez learned to read. The French brought education to remote villages for the first time. His father, 'Ali was able to secure Hafez a place, making him the first of his children to start formal education, being a few of the fortunate boys in his village to be so lucky.

Al-Assad's family belonged to the Alawite branch of Shi'i Islam. It was a remnant of the Shi'i upsurge that had swept Islam a thousand years back. They held to the Shia belief that 'Ali, the Prophet Muhammad's cousin and son-in-law, was his rightful heir, but was robbed of this by the first three Caliphs. They also believed in reincarnation, which most Muslims sects did not believe. This and their other esoteric beliefs were denounced by Sunni Orthodox Muslims which added with the repression throughout the centuries made the Alawites more secretive about their religion.

The event which Hafez called as ''the crucial point in his life' came in 1939-1940 when he was nine and his parents sent him away from the mountains to a school in Latakia on the coast. He spent the first three months with his sister, but after her sister had to move somewhere else, he was put in a humble lodging-house owned by a family acquaintance. For him, this was a sad period in his life, because of the distance from his family. He said that – ''In those days the thirty kilometres from Qurdaha to Latakia seemed almost as great as the distance between Damascus and London''. But he remembered it also it joyfully, because of the children that he ran about the town. It was a challenge for a child of the mountains to be thrown into urban life.

Most importantly he felt for a first time what it was like being a member of an ill-regarded minority. Alawites were not well placed in Latakia at that time, which was then about three-quarters Sunni Muslim and the other made up of different Christian sects and denominations. Alawites were few, perhaps only in hundreds. They had little influence in the city and were sneered at. They did their best to keep out of trouble and lived in the poorer areas of the town and naturally, Hafez was quite homesick. He lived there at a dramatic moment. Syria was then under the control of Vichy France, who lived in fear of a British attack, which did not come until the summer of 1941. But as Assad said himself, he was not that much worried about the Second World War, but more about his homework.

He did well in school and won several certificates of merit, which he presented to his father when he came back home in the summer of

1940. In that narrow setting, he had already distinguished himself. In 1942, Assad was one of only four other boys from his village who sat the examinations for a primary school certificate. It was a vital hurdle on the way to secondary education. Before the examinations, their headmaster told them not to be scared by the sight of unfamiliar teachers in a Western dress who spoke both French and Arabic. And they also told them that they are ''as good as the town boys''. They went into the exam with these words in their heads and the headmaster was right as their results proved to be among the best.

Hafez inherited an important legacy from his father and grandfather, which was that he was born into a family which was vigorously bettering themselves at a time when the

Alawite community as a whole was emerging from its long neglect. His grandfather's muscular legacy was an important clue to Assad's character. From this time on, the Alawite community did not defer or knuckle under and were not easily punched around. His father's contribution was even more prominent for his family. He gave his son an education, which earned him self-respect and respect of others. In 1936, an official document listed 'Ali Sulayman as *chef alaouite* or head of a clan, although his position in the list indicated that he occupied a lesser place than the leading dignitaries of the community. A 1942 survey of Alawite tribes and clans, which was made by the wartime British political Officer showed 'Ali Sulayman's family to be the head of the minor al-'A'ila clan of the Kalbiya tribe, which was a modest eminence, but a real one.

To his father's influence, Hafez owed a lifelong interest in books, poetry and the Arabic language. Developing a good memory became something of a family tradition. One day, when he was in his teens, his father challenged him and one of his brothers to a memory competition: who would be the first to learn a long poem by Hassan Ibn Thabit (a friend of Prophet Muhammad who followed him into a battle and commemorated his deeds in verse). After the poem was copied out, the boys went out of doors to study it. Hafez came back first but found that his father had already closed the book and was ready to recite. In Assad's later years, his elephantine powers of recall were a source of uneasy admiration among his staff. It was also remarked that his accomplished use of classical Arabic, especially off-the-cut speeches, distinguished him in public life.

Because of his education and his vigorous personality, Hafez was soon seen as the heir to Sulayman and 'Ali Sulayman. By the time Hafez was twenty-five years old, his father was eighty years old and he came to assume some of the family responsibilities. In particular, he helped his mother with two of his youngest brothers – Jamil and Rif'at, who being less serious and single-minded, regarded Hafez as a somewhat stern father-figure whose approval they sought, but whose authority they liked to challenge. Hafez al-Assad was the first member of his family to leave the world of Qurdaha behind. His parents, aunts, uncles, cousins and half-brothers remained rooted in the village, but from an early age, he was out of his own, learning to think for himself and acquiring interests and ambitions beyond their horizon.

Hafez al-Assad's father, Ali Sulayman al-Assad.

Chapter 2 – The Student

In Assad's secondary school class, some of his classmates came from the higher classes. They were the children of the landowners, the merchants, the financiers and the religious dignitaries. They could trace their prominence to the older Ottoman rule, which the French did little to disturb. Assad did not have fond memories of those kids, whom he remembered as bullies. He said that they used to beat up the boys they did not like and would go to Abu 'Ali's food shop to eat and feed their friends, while the poor boys could only look at them and be hungry. They would change their clothes once a week, which was a sign of exceptional wealth, while the less fortunate went to school in rags and couldn't even afford to buy books.

Rich boys did not even bother to work, but simply gave themselves what marks they wanted at the end of the year and very few teachers dared to stand up to them. 'Alawi mountain boys like Assad studied hard because they knew that getting into secondary school was a struggle in itself and had no thought of throwing away the change to better themselves.

There was one teacher whom Assad even forty years later regarded as a hero. It was in 1945, that after failing to control the boys, especially an insolent youth whose smart clothes marked him out as a son of a rich family, who joked among his cronies and refused to sit down without any respect for the teacher, that he bundled all of his papers with trembling hands and said – ''You

can't buy my dignity for a few liras''
and walked out being aware that his
salary was paid by the fathers of
those rich boys such as the one who
was tormenting him.

After many talks, Syria attained full
independence in 1946 when the last
French troops left the country. During
this time, a full battle of ideas raged
in Syria with many parties and
ideologies competing to attain
power. The richer, wealthier and
conservative families such those
discussed above supported the
Muslim Brotherhood. It was a Sunni
Islamist party, who wanted to fight
against the westernisation of Syrian
society and to purify Islam from
foreign influence. When the
constitution was being written, they
failed to win the backing which would
have made Islam the state religion.

There were many other parties, such as the Peoples Party, which was pro-western compared to the National Party, which was pro-Eastern.

On the other side existed other parties. The main three were the: Syrian Communist Party, Syrian National Socialist Party (SSNP) and the Syrian Ba'athist party. All of them would have been much more attractive to the minorities in Syria as all of them were secular, but with differences. The Communist Party was quite small because the industrial proletariat was not big enough to form a powerful political base. Khaled Baqdash was the leader of the party, who was a very talented Kurdish lawyer from Damascus. Kurds heavily backed the party. Women were also important supporters of the party, because of their support for women's rights. The Communists sought to form alliances with the other left-wing movements to extend their influence. Syrian National Socialist Party was formed in 1932 by Antoun Saadeh, who was an Orthodox Christian who had a strong personal charisma and sought to form a Greater Syria, which he believed should extend from the Taurus Mountains across the Sinai Desert to the Suez Canal and the Red Sea, as well as eastwards to the Zagros Mountains, which form the border between Iraq and Iran, then down to the Persian Gulf. His was a territorial based nationalism. He also added Cyprus to this national homeland. Antoun Saadeh believed that there was an unbreakable, indivisible link between those lands and its people, which he said were all the descendants of the glorious ancient civilisations who inhabited those areas. Therefore, his party rejected Islam and the Arabic language as a source of nationhood, and it was not a pan-Arab movement. Saadeh would be later executed in 1949 in Lebanon as Lebanese government saw his ideas a threat to the Lebanese independence.

Although they were competitors with the Ba'ath party and their importance would decrease in 1950's, they were not prohibited after the Ba'ath takeover in 1963 and would be part of an alliance called the National Progressive Front, with each party having a few seats in the legislative body, the People's Council and the executive body, the Council of Ministers.

The Ba'th Party was founded in 1946 by Michel Aflaq and Salah al-Din al-

Bitar. It excited the minds of a whole generation. They believed that the Arabs had sunk by the early twentieth century. After enduring four decades of Turkish rule, they witnessed Syria under the French losing territories both to Turkey and Israel. Aflaq formulated a theory and a programme to rouse the Arabs from what he considered a living death. This is what he meant by *Ba'ath.* The core of the theory was that the Arabs had every reason to feel proud since they belonged to the Arab race with many glorious achievements to its credit. The Arab nation, Aflaq taught, was millennial, eternal and unique, stretching back into the mists of time and forward to a brighter future. To express his belief in the unity of Arab history, the Ba'ath founder coined the phrase: ''One Arab nation with an eternal message''. He opposed tribalism, sectarianism, the oppression of women and the supremacy of landowners and sought to break them up. He also coined a three-word guide to action: 'Unity, Freedom, Socialism'. Unity sought to bond all Arabs back together. Freedom meant freedom from foreign domination, but also from mental and social chains. Socialism was the Ba'ath answer to the concentration of wealth and power in the hands of the higher classes and much else that was exploitative in Syrian society. But their socialism was nationalist socialism instead of an internationalist. Aflaq asserted that Islam was an Arab religion, which offended devout Muslims, by suggesting that Islam was a flowering of Arab genius rather than the revelation of God, while he also annoyed his fellow Christians who accused him to selling out to the other side. By deferring to Islam, he also countered the preaching of the Muslim Brotherhood, who with their Golden Age vision of a purged Islamic state, had gone to war against secular parties, such as the Ba'ath and were his most dangerous rivals.

In 1946, at the age of sixteen, Assad took a side in the political debate and joined the Ba'ath. By this time, he was already seen as confident, combative, class-conscious and unashamed of his background. He was physically robust, no doubt a gift from his grandfather's genes and could hold his own in the rough and tumble of the schoolyard, where he was not afraid to stand up the higher-class bullies. He became a party stalwart and defended its cause on the street. He wrote leaflets and distributed them, on one occasion planting them inside an army barracks. This feat was never attempted before and it earned him great admiration from all.

In 1949, the whole Assad family moved from their native Qurdaha to Latakia to look after their eldest son Ri'fat who was then starting secondary school. They took rooms in a lodging house from where they had a ringside view of their elder son's political activities. His mother was more sympathetic than his father, who like many men of his generation, saw ideological parties as dangerously subversive. By 1951, the Ba'ath had outgrown both the Communists and the Syrian Nationalists and were competing against the fundamentalist Muslim

Brotherhood, who were in alliance with the city's elites. The Brotherhood had picked out Assad as one of the student leaders and repeatedly tried to beat him up. Mahmud 'Ujayl who later became a member of the People's Assembly, fought shoulder to shoulder with Assad in these brawls. In 1948, members of the Muslim Brotherhood caught Assad on his own and knifed him in the back. The wound took several weeks to heal. By this time, he started to seek out Sunni alliances to reach across the Alawite-Sunni divide, which would become a characteristic of his adult politics.

In his last two years at school, 1949-1951, Assad was elected head of his school's student affairs committee and was acknowledged as a schoolboy-politician. During this time,

Assad struck out important friendships that would last to adulthood. One of them was 'Abd al-Rauf al-Kasm, who was a Sunni from a religious family and would serve as Assad's longest-serving Prime Minister.

In 1951, Hafez al-Assad was elected President of the nation-wide Union of Syrian Students, which was important for him, his community and his party. This is proof that by this time, he was the most important schoolboy of the day. Importantly, he considered himself a politician first and foremost, even later when wearing the uniform of Syria's air force. His many struggles against the Communist, pan-Syrians and the whole of the right with the Muslim Brotherhood would give him political education and informed his attitudes to movements which forty years were still present in the Syrian political scene. He looked back at his youth as a time of heroism and selfless duty in the nationalist and socialist cause, and this was the model he was to recommend to subsequent generations of young people. The early fights in the streets became part of the legitimacy he later claimed.

Michel Aflaq, founder of the Ba'ath Party and the architect of the party's ideology.

Chapter 3 – The Pilot

The 1950s in Syria was an era of political instability with the country frequently changing its system of government. In 1948, in the Mandate of Palestine, Zionist militias began taking control over as much of the country as they could. Palestinian society, which was badly unprepared and uncoordinated collapsed, immediately angering Syria and other Arab states and causing large numbers of Palestinians to flee. Syria was involved in the 1947-1949 Arab-Israeli War and after Israeli victory, it was the last country to sign an armistice with the country which occurred in July 1949. It occurred after 1949 March coup d'etat which overthrew Syria's democratically elected government with the alleged help of the United States and CIA.

Then in the same year in 1949, there were coups inside the coup with the first leader Husni al-Za'im overthrown with Sami al-Hinnawi and finally by Adib al-Shishakli. In 1951, he completely took over the country, but because of the growing opposition, Shishakli resigned in 1954 and left the country and parliamentary rule was restored in Syria with factions favouring strong relations with the Soviet Union. During the Suez Crisis martial law was implemented in Syria and Syrian and Iraqi troops were put in Jordan to prevent a possible Israeli invasion. In 1958, Syria merged with Egypt and formed the United Arab Republic, with all Syrian parties, including the Ba'ath ceasing their activities, as this was one of the Egyptian conditions for the merger. Because of Egyptian dominance, discontent grew and in

1961 elements against the Union took power and the Republic dissolved, restoring Syrian independence. However, instability continued with military revolts, coups, riots and disorders being a part of life in the early 1960s. Finally, in the 8th of March 1963, a coup engineered by the Ba'ath party and National Council of the Revolutionary Command (NCRC) took power with one of the founders of the Ba'ath party Salah al-Din al-Bitar becoming Prime Minister and also bringing Hafez al-Assad to power.

After he finished school, Assad wanted to be a doctor, which would have been a big leap into the professional middle class. His father agreed and Assad telephoned to Beirut, to the Jesuit Academy of St Joseph to ask if he could enrol in its medical facility. But he was told that there had to be many papers to fill and that he had to come to Beirut himself. But because the family had little cash to spare, he had to choose another direction for himself. He chose the army as it was an attractive option for him because fees had been abolished and the lower class boys felt that it was a good place to start their careers, especially after the 1949 coups brought it to power, which made ideological parties encourage their young members to join it in hope of taking control. Therefore in 1950, Assad joined the Syrian Armed Forces. He liked the idea of flying and wanted to do it and in the same year entered a flying school in Aleppo. He much preferred days spent flying rather than the other military side as for him it was more fun and he saw it as a holiday.

Assad came out on top in his class and on graduation won a trophy for aerobatics. He found great freedom in flying and he admitted it was more fun than in the later years for the other air force cadets because in Assad's time the rules were less important, the technology was not as developed and, because of that there was no radar or ground control and nobody knew where they were. He told how he would fly to his native Qurdaha to show off to his friends and family and then find himself over the Mediterranean.

On the eve of his graduation day in 1955, Assad narrowly escaped disaster. At the rehearsal, two formations of four aircraft were due to fly past and land in turn. As Assad's formation wheeled to allow the plane behind to come in, it entered a dense cloud over Aleppo. To fly blind required a skill, which Assad did not yet possess. He knew he had to watch his instruments and not trust his senses. He noticed he was losing speed and opened the throttle, but he was surprised that the speedometer needle continued to fall. He felt that the engine was vibrating, and dust was falling in his eyes. Only then did he realise that he was flying upside down. He shot out of the cloud and found himself heading straight to the earth. He said – 'Just in time I managed to climb to safety, grazing the tops of the olive trees. Other cadets watching me said ''Has he gone mad''?''. They thought I was playing games, but I wasn't'. The next day, Assad graduated and collected his cup for aerobatics.

Hafez al-Assad standing above with fellow cadets, 1951-1952.

On his graduation day, Assad as a pilot officer was posted to the Mezze airbase near Damascus. This inevitably plunged him into the political intrigues of the time. In the early 1950s, the Syrian officer corps was the most politicised and faction-ridden in the Arab world. When Shishakli was overthrown and party life was restored, the way was open for more active political infighting. Assad too embarked on an attempt to win over brother officers and bring himself to the party headquarters. His first discovery was that the tensions and conflicts inside the officer's corps mirrored the battles he had fought at school. Although some flirted with communism, the main fault-line was between the Ba'ath and the Saadeh's pan-Syrian nationalists. In 1955, Assad was chosen to go to Egypt for further instruction. Cairo, which was the seat of Gamal Abdal Nasser's revolutionary government, was a stirring place to be heading for. After the 1948 defeat and the loss of Palestine, the Arabs were demoralised until the charismatic Nasser emerged on the scene. Assad played little drama during the Suez Crisis, when Nasser nationalised the Suez Canal Company in angry response the West's withdrawal of aid promised for the Aswan High Dam. During this time, the Arab enthusiasm knew no bounds. Syria offered to fight for Egypt, when three months later Britain and France, in secret collusion with Israel invaded Egypt, but knowing that militarily his cause was doomed, Nasser declined. Assad had returned to Syria in early 1956, and during the Suez crisis, he was sent north to the Nayrab base near Aleppo to fly reconnaissance missions over northern and eastern Syria.

Egyptian President Gamel Abdel Nasser waving to crowds in Mansoura, 1960.

On return from his training course in Egypt, Assad had fallen in love with Aniseh Makhluf, a girl he had known since childhood and whom he hand singled out when he was in his early twenties. She was a distant relation as his Aunt Sa'da had married into the Makhluf family. It was a connection that allowed Assad to pay many visits to Aniseh's home village of Bustan al-Basha. She was a schoolteacher of demure good manners, a trim dark-haired young woman of about his age, who had been most respectably educated at the French-run Convent of the Sacred Heart at Banyas on the coast. Aniseh had an independent mind of her own and was a good judge of character. After some doubts of Aniseh's family, due to their richer status and pan-Syrian leanings, which clashed with Assad's Ba'athist beliefs, Assad prevailed, and the couple married in Damascus in front of a *qadi* or religious notary. In the first years of their marriage, Assad could not afford the standard of living, that she had been used to, but neither this nor the ups and downs of the army and political life appear to have daunted her. She was to prove a devoted wife and mother and Assad's closest and most trusted confidante, providing him with a domestic environment of unquestioned respectability. Although it was a love match, marriage brought Assad into the respected Makhluf clan, helping him rise to a higher social level. It won him points in the 'Alawi community and contributed to his growing self-confidence.

In 1958, Assad was chosen to go to the Soviet Union for a course in night flying in MiG-15s and MiG-17s which were newly delivered to Syria. He was given an emotional send-off by his family and friends, for whom not so long before travelling down the mountain from Qurdaha to Latakia had seemed a momentous leap. As he later recalled, 'In those days people said goodbye to you as if you would never return'. Aniseh, already pregnant, went home to wait for him in Bustan al-Basha. The voyage to Russia was Assad's first contact with a country which was to be the principal ally of his presidency. He learned some Russian, but he and other officers were very homesick during their stay, therefore they pleaded with their Soviet instructors to allow them to work overtime to finish their course early. He stayed there for 10 months until he returned to Syria in the spring of 1959. Assad hastened up the mountains to see his wife and the baby daughter born in his absence. But a shock awaited him when he reported back to duty. The Officer's Club, which lately had been the hub of politics in the city, had been shorn of all importance, while the offices of the Ba'ath party were deserted. The two ladders of his ambitions had been kicked away from under him.

Nasser's conditions for uniting with Syria were that the Syrian army should withdraw from politics and the political parties be dissolved. However, the officers and the civilian Ba'ath leaders did not understand that Nasser would exclude them from the union, which they had created. In place of the rich tumult of Syrian politics, Nasser erected a structure which was both authoritarian and unstable. In Damascus, his power depended on Colonel Abdel Hamid al-Sarraj, whom he promoted Minister of the Interior. Syria lost all its independence and the Syrians were disappointed, who had once welcomed Nasser in Damascus like a new Saladin.

In late, 1959, Assad's squadron was transferred to Cairo. During these times of disgruntlement, Assad and his friends grew to distrust the Ba'ath founders – Aflaq and Bitar, who they believed had sacrificed the party by dismantling it without consulting its rank and file. Assad later said – 'We came to distrust their commitment to the Ba'athist ideals we had grown up with. We felt they had been trading in slogans'. Assad and his friends now convinced themselves that Aflaq and Bitar had secretly welcomed the party's demise because it served to silence criticism welling up from more radical forces below. This resentment would lead to a 1966 Ba'ath schism when it split into a Syrian and an Iraqi faction. It would be in the Iraqi faction that Aflaq would take refuge. The Syrian Officers, including Assad, would come to believe that Nasser was being manipulated by a clique as corrupt as the ones he had once ousted. During this atmosphere of gloom and doom, Assad and four fellow officers embarked on an enterprise which was to change the course of Syrian history.

Early in 1960, the five officers, one of them being Assad, founded a secret organisation they called the 'Military Committee''. Three of them were Alawites while the other two came from another Shi'i offshoot –

Isma'ilis. All of them had sworn
loyalty to each other. The Isma'ilis
were 'Abd al-Karim al-Jundi and
Ahmad al-Mir. The two other
Alawites were Muhammad 'Umran
and Salah Jadid. In the future, Jadid
would become Assad's main
competitor for power. In 1961, the
United Arab Republic dissolved. It
was a right-wing coup, backed by
Jordan and Saudi Arabia and the
disgruntled Syrian business
community. Nasser's July 1961
nationalisation decrees were the
main reason which triggered the
coup. It was headed by Lieutenant
Colonel Abd al-Karim al-Nahlawi.
Nasser decided not to intervene and
his Field-Marshal 'Amer was put on a
plane to Cairo and other unwanted
Egyptians were repatriated. Before
the disunion, the Military Committee
hoped to better the situation and

save the Union, but with no luck. The break-up put Assad and his colleagues in jail. He was later released and repatriated in exchange for a group of Egyptian officers detained in Syria. During that time, Assad's wife and their second daughter were escorted back to Syria. Their first daughter had gotten sick earlier, hurting Assad very much. In 1962, a failed coup took place in which Assad played a minor role and was jailed in Lebanon but later repatriated. By that year, Assad had become a full-time conspirator and the Military Committee were preparing to take power.

Chapter 4 – The Revolutionary

On 8th of February 1963, Assad and his friends woke up to the great news that their Ba'ath party comrades in Iraq had overthrown and killed the Iraqi leader, 'Abd al-Karim Qasim. The overthrown of Qasim was a big victory for the Ba'athists and put the Ba'ath on a par with Nasser. The Military Committee decided to mount their coup on 7th of March, just a month after the Iraqis. But just before the coup would have begun, the Military Intelligence raided the apartment where the planners were assembling. Some officers were arrested, and others went into hiding. Because of the inadequate communications, Assad had to get the message out that the coup had been put back by twenty-four hours.

The coup occurred swiftly on the
night of 7-8 March. Assad's moment
of glory was the capture of Dumayr
airbase east of Damascus. Later that
morning, the coup-makers assembled
at army headquarters to celebrate
their lightning victory. The coup was
nearly bloodless and was greeted by
the indifference by the population. A
week earlier, Assad and the others
lived a shadowy and precarious life
with hardly a telephone or a
motorcar between them. Now they
were the strongest force in Syrian
politics. Their revolution had
succeeded. Assad was promoted
lieutenant-colonel and was named
commander of the Dumayr airbase.
Their first task was to invest power in
a secret-twenty-man National Council
for the Revolutionary Command
(NCRC). It was composed of twelve
Ba'athists, eight Nasserites and

independents, which reflected the factions which had come together to overthrow the previous Syrian government. Assad became in all but name the real boss of the air force, which for a man in his thirties was a big promotion as he was just a captain a day before. He also did not neglect self-improvement as it was noticed that he kept a volume of Arabic philology on his desk at the airbase.

Because they were still too junior to present themselves to the public as Syrian leaders, they appointed Amin al-Hafiz to the critical post of Minister of the Interior. He would also become President and until 1966 would sometimes hold the post of the Prime Minister. Hafiz was a Sunni, the son of an Aleppo policeman, who had volunteered for service in the 1948

Palestine war. In 1954, he joined the uprising against Shishakli and was promoted to command the Eastern Front at Deir ez-Zor and then to be commandant of the Homs academy, before being posted to Cairo. After the relations with Egypt broke down, he was sent back to Damascus. Later in December 1961, he was exiled to Buenos Aires as a military attaché, and it was from there that he was summoned back to Syria by the victorious officers after the 8 March coup. He had nothing to do with either the party or the Military Committee. The Military Committee wanted him to front for them and pulled the necessary strings.

Although Ba'athism and Nasserism were similar and had the same pan-Arab goals, the sides would not be able to work together for long. On

July 18, 1963, the Nasserites attempt at a coup failed. On July 22nd, Nasser denounced the Ba'athists which ended the hopes of a possible Ba'ath-Nasserite coalition and strengthened Ba'ath power. Damascus now took in hand its own destinies for the first time since independence, and from these complicated and violent beginnings, it was in due course to grow into a leading regional power.

After the consolidation, because of the Military Committee's distrust of Aflaq and Bitar, they turned to the Marxist faction which some Ba'athists had formed after the party's dissolution. This group of thinkers was led by Hammud al-Shufi who was a Druze schoolteacher of thirty-six whom voracious reading of socialist literature and harsh jail experience during the union years had converted

into a staunch left-winger. The
Military Committee and Shufi's
Marxists joined forces and together
dominated the Ba'ath party's
Regional Congress of September
1963 at which Shufi was elected
secretary and Assad a member of a
new eight-man Regional Command.
Neither Aflaq nor Bitar, who
sometimes was Prime Minister of the
country, were included. Assad,
although not yet known to the public,
began debating policies and theories
and taking decisions, which was an
enriching experience. He situated
himself on the left, but this was more
of a gut feeling, rather than a
theoretical commitment as coming
from a minority he felt sympathy for
the downtrodden who had been at
odds with the Sunni establishment
for a millennium.

Although strongly on the left, Assad was not a communist. Khalid al-Fahum, a Palestinian on the pro-Syrian side of the PLO (Palestine Liberation Organisation) politics, remember calling on him in a small bare office at Air Force Headquarters on Baghdad Street. Fahum was anxious to learn where the new leaders stood, especially on Palestine. Assad, he concluded was certainly 'left' as he hated the city bosses and their rural allies and sided unreservedly with the peasanty of his home province. But he was not a Communist. Fahum noted that Assad saw no difference between a Syrian and a Palestinian and seemed a committed Arab nationalist.

Assad was entrusted with the most important security job of the regime. The officers realised that to protect the army from factionalism that had dominated it since independence was to make it a Ba'ath monopoly. As Assad later said it, the goal was to create an 'ideological army', which would be in stark contrast with the 'army in politics' of the past. Assad sought the help of an Aflaq's early rival, the philosopher Zaki al-Arsuzi. Arsuzi contributed frequent editorials to the party and the army press and gave Assad ideological insights which were important to his development at this time. In due course, Assad arranged Arsuzi to receive a pension which he kept until his death in Damascus on 2 July 1968. 'He lived a poor man and died as one, but he was respected by all who knew him' was Assad's epitaph. Meanwhile, Assad went about his work of bringing every unit under the close control of the Military Committee by ensuring that loyalists occupied the sensitive commands and that the political education of the troops was not neglected. His grassroots knowledge of the armed services was to contribute to his later ascendancy.

The high Ba'ath optimism of the summer of 1963 ended in November when the Ba'ath was put out of power in Iraq and President Abdul Salam Arif made peace with Nasser. Sheer survival rather than Arab conquest was now the Ba'ath's priority. The sudden slump in the party's quarrels and fortunes caused Aflaq and the officers to forget their quarrels and brought them into a tactical alliance against the Marxists. In February 1964 the Marxists were expelled from the party together with their supporters at emergency Regional and National congresses.

However, dropping the Marxists did not help the Ba'ath. Seeing the infighting in the party, its enemies rose against it, hoping that it could bring down the regime. In early 1964, prayer-leaders preached inflammatory sermons against the secular, socialist Ba'ath. The centre of the insurrection was Hama, which was a stronghold of landed conservatism and the Muslim Brotherhood. Hostility between the Ba'ath and the Muslim Brotherhood that Assad had witnessed in the 1940s and the 1950s had not ended, and they would until their crushing in 1982 be the main opposition to the Ba'ath rule in Syria. During the insurrection, they ransacked wine shops to spill the offending liquor into the gutters and beat up any party member they could find. One of them was a young militiaman of the

Ba'ath's National Guard, an Isma'ili called Munzir al-Shimali who was killed and mutilated. On the party's Regional Command, Assad had joined in the decisions to put down the troubles and prove to Hama who was in charge. The uprising was suppressed. In their first eighteen months, the Military Committee has weathered three crises: clash with the Nasserites, the rout of the Ba'athists in Iraq and the Hama insurrection.

But quarrels in the party continued. It culminated in the 1966 Syrian coup d'etat, when the ruling National Command of the Ba'ath party were removed from power by a union of the party's Military Committee and the Regional Command. The main political casualties were the Minister of Defence Muhammad Umran who was jailed, Prime Minister Salah al-Din al-Bitar who later fled to Beirut, President Amin al-Hafiz who was jailed, then fled to Beirut, Lebanon and later Iraq and Michel Aflaq who would live out his exile in Iraq. This finally cemented a split of the Ba'ath between a Syrian faction and an Iraqi faction.

The coup gave the thirty-five-year-old Assad his first seat in the Syrian cabinet. He was made Minister of Defence, which thrust him at once into the forefront of the Syrian Israeli confrontation. The new government was the most radical Syria had ever seen. It sought to overturn Syria's social, political and economic structures. Salah Jadid was the head of the new government. He was forty years old, polite, soft-spoken and usually dressed in civilian clothes. He was by nature discreet and did not seem to enjoy human contact. He rarely appeared in public or made speeches.

The left-wing Ba'athist government had improved life for the lower classes. It enabled many people to get on in life in ways which would have once been impossible. For example, in Raqqa in the late 1960s, the head of a local branch of the Peasant's Union was the son of the slave of a local tribal chieftain. And the party secretary for the province was a schoolteacher whose father had been a vegetable seller. Although the Ba'athists had not lost its suspicion of communism, for the first time in Syrian history, a Communist Samih 'Atiyya entered the government as Minister of Communications.

In late 1966, Salim Hatum tried to overthrow the Jadid government. Jadid was put on house arrest and Hatum planned to kill him. But Assad learned about the coup and ordered the 70th Brigade to the city. Hatum and his supporters fled to Jordan. Jadid was very thankful for Assad and Assad earned Jadid's gratitude.

Salah Jadid.

Chapter 5 – The Number Two

The year of 1967 was not a happy one for Syria and other Arab states. The defeat by Israel in the Six-Day War made Jordan lose the West Bank and East Jerusalem, Egypt the Gaza Strip and the Sinai Peninsula and Syria the Golan Heights to Israel. During this time, Assad was unable to sleep and fainted with fatigue at the Defence Ministry. When the immediate danger was over, he went home and wrestled over the catastrophe for three days, refusing to see anyone. Several party members demanded Assad's immediate resignation. It was defeated by one vote. These dreadful days would become a catalyst for Assad's rise to the position of Number One.

Before the war, Assad did not show that the was ambitious and that was probably his greatest asset as he did not arouse suspicion. The defeat spurred into him an ambition to rule Syria free from the constraints of colleagues and rivals who he felt had driven the country to disaster. During this time, he began building a personal power base in the military and forged loyalty to himself by distributing favours and rendering services and continuously furthered the careers of friends like the tank officer Mustafa Tlas, who would later become the Minister of Defence.

The Syrian government refused to accept Security Council Resolution 242 of 22 November 1967 which proposed that Israel should trade territories seized in the war for peace. It denounced it as a betrayal of Palestinian rights. The war convinced Assad that expansionism was Israel's very nature and that an immense Arab effort would be required to contain it. But he had no patience with bluster which served to isolate Syria from much of the rest of the world.

The disagreements which began with Assad and his colleagues in 1967 became more acute the following year. Assad's main priority was fixed on the military conquest with Israel, whereas Jadid preferred to keep attention on domestic matters and his vision of a socialist revolution. Assad preferred opening the party to new members, while Jadid did not because he was afraid that opportunists, rather than ideologues would join. Assad also preferred to open relations with Iraq, where the

Ba'ath had regained power in the 17 July 1968 coup. During this time, Assad extended his grip on the army, but Jadid still dominated the party apparatus. During the Regional and National Party Congresses of September and October 1968, Assad was outvoted on most issues and his arguments were rejected. However, by the end of 1968, Assad had already outstripped Jadid in the accumulation of power. His manoeuvrings in the army – postings, transfers, sackings and re-recruitments threw Jadid on the defensive. Dr Munif al-Razzaz, who was a civilian party leader who had himself been deposed by Jadid in 1966 commented that 'Jadid's fatal mistake was to attempt to govern the army through the party'.

But Jadid still controlled the security

and intelligence services through
'Abd al-Karim al-Jundi. He was the
head of the party's Bureau of
National Security from September
1967. He was able to create an
atmosphere of terror where petty
informers were recruited, and
arbitrary arrests became frequent.
Few dared to go about in the capital
after dark for fear of being stopped
by the security police and taken
away. People were even reluctant to
leave the country because security
agencies were known to confiscate
empty houses. Much of this was
linked with the name of Jundi. The
conflict between Assad and Jundi
erupted in February 1969 when the
two rivals chose to pitch their dispute
in policy terms and their respective
supporters came to blows. On the
level of gun and fist, the contest was
waged between Assad's combative

young brother Rif'at and Jadid's security chief Jundi. Rif'at had joined the Ba'ath party in 1952 and in 1965 was appointed deputy commander of a special party security force.

Rif'at came to believe that Jadid was planning an attack on Assad's life. A car driver who lurked near Assad's house had confessed under interrogation that he had been sent by Jundi to assassinate him. The evidence could not be checked, but Rif'at argued that unless Jundi was disarmed, the Assad brothers were themselves at risk. In the four days 25-28 February, the two brothers carried out something just short of a coup. Tanks were moved to key points in Damascus. Government and party newspaper editors who were loyal to Jadid were ousted and replaced by Assad's men. Vehicles of

Jundi's security service were in the habit of filling up with petrol in the Ministry of Defence compound. This gave Rif'at the idea of arresting each driver as he came in. In this way, Jundi was stripped of his fleet of jeeps, but only when his chauffeur was taken did, he realise his time was up. In the night of 1-2 March, after a violent telephone altercation with the head of the Military Intelligence 'Ali Dhadha, Jundi committed suicide by shooting himself in the head.

Jundi's death caused a change in the balance of power. It consecrated Rif'at as Assad's strong right arm in internal conflicts. Although Assad did not press his advantage and allowed Jadid to keep his position, Assad's policies gained a footing. Class struggle was toned down, criticism of other Arab regimes was muted, and some political prisoners were released. At about this time Assad and Nureddin al-Atassi called on Nasser in Cairo. Nasser had found out about the political fights in Syria and said 'Ah, you Ba'athists. You're so harsh with each other! When we in Egypt formed our Free Officers movement, we agreed that if we ever fell out, each of us would be free to return to private life.' Like in many other things, the Syrians were not ready to follow Egypt in this example. Of the five founding members of the Military Committee, one was dead, two were in exile and only two remained: Assad and Jadid, who were locked in a power struggle where only one would survive.

Nureddin al-Atassi (on the left) and Assad (in the middle) meeting with Nasser (on the right).

During the time of 1969-1970, turbulent events caused Assad and Jadid to focus away from their narrow power struggle. During this time 'duality of power' existed between the two. The instability in the region where Jordan conflicted with PLO where the new Yaser Arafat was in charge led Salah Jadid to send Syrian troops into Jordan in the hope

of overthrowing the monarchy and
assisting the PLO. It would be
remembered as Black September.
Assad disobeyed Jadid's orders to
launch airstrikes into Jordan for the
fear that Israel would intervene
against Syria. This was the beginning
of the end of Assad's long coup to
fully overthrow Jadid. Nasser would
later negotiate an end to the civil war
and would die soon after on the 28th
of September 1970.

By September 1970, Assad had
informally taken power in Syria but
he waited several more weeks before
advancing to the front of the stage.
When an Algerian diplomat Lakhdar
Brahimi was dining with the Head of
State, Dr Atasi, he said to Lakhdar -
'Don't discuss serious matters with
me. Assad is in charge'. During the
National Party Congress, Assad

derided his radical critics. As the
congress ended, Jadid's supporters,
fearing that Assad would move to
arrest them, became increasingly
distraught. On 12th of November
1970, Assad ordered his loyalists to
arrest the main members of Jadid's
government. Salah Jadid is said to
have refused and said – 'If I ever take
power, you will be dragged through
the streets until you die'. Assad
consigned Jadid to the grim fortress
of Mezze prison, where he would be
imprisoned until his death. His
brother Rif'at took charge of security
in the capital. On November 16, while
Assad was finishing his takeover, the
Libyan leader Muammar Gaddafi,
who had heard the news and wanted
to see what was going had landed
unannounced at the Damascus
Airport. Assad went to meet him at
the airport and joked – 'It's a good

thing you didn't arrive half an hour earlier'. Iraqis, who detested the Jadid regime were happy about the coup, although Michel Aflaq and Amin al-Hafiz would have preferred to have seen all members of the Military Committee consigned to oblivion. During that time Assad's wife Aniseh had a dream where she was standing in the middle of a large crowd of people looking in the same direction. Following their gaze, she saw in the distance a square object which, as she came closer, turned out to be a box with a peephole in one side of it. She put her eye to the hole and there was the Al-Asqa Mosque in Jerusalem, one of Islam's holiest shrines. She picked up the box, turned around and found her husband standing behind her and handed it to him. This meant, she told him that morning – 'that you will triumph over your enemies and become the strongest of all Arab leaders'.

Chapter 6 – The Leader

Hafez al-Assad came to rule Syria with an instant advantage because the Jadid's regime he replaced was so detested that any alternative came as a relief. Because he was more liberal than Salah Jadid, his victory ushered in a political honeymoon as people were longing to breathe more freely. Ordinary people soon had reasons to be thankful for Assad's accession. The price of basic foods was cut by 15 per cent. The hated security services were purged and curbed, while responsibility for dealing with many crimes was transferred from the army to the police. Restrictions on travel and trade with Lebanon were lifted which restored Syrians their natural space. Also, assurances were given to the private sector, and exiles and emigrants were encouraged to bring home their money and skills. At first, when the Ba'ath first came to power in 1963, Assad was at the forefront of the drive to break the city's hold over the countryside. But by 1970, and with ambitious economic and military plans in mind, Assad knew he needed allies in the urban middle class, so breaking with his political past, he tried to win over the shopkeepers, businessmen and artisans of the towns. This Assad's revolution would become known as the ''Corrective Movement''.

Hafez al-Assad, shortly after coming to power, 1970.

After coming to power, Assad had two basic ideas about how to govern Syria. The first was that there could be no challenge to his rule and the second was that popular backing for his policies was nevertheless necessary. On the domestic front his key idea was that, unless Syria was itself united, there could be no hope of joint Arab action and therefore no hope of recovering territories from Israel. When pictures of Assad started to appear in the public they were welcomed by the common people, who had distrusted the faceless collegiality of the previous regime. Yet for a person being from a minority religious group – Alawite, ruling Syria so openly demanded courage. Salah Jadid had not been so brave as he had chosen the Sunni Atassi to front for him, in a tacit admission that membership of a heterodox sect on the outer limits of Shi'ism was a political handicap. On overthrowing Jadid, Assad, in turn, seemed to hesitate on the threshold of the top job, contenting himself at first with the title of Prime Minister and putting forward as head of state a little-known Sunni schoolteacher of thirty-nine Ahmad al-Khatib. But his early doubts were not in keeping with his character and convictions, as from boyhood he had tried to free himself from sectarian complexes. Therefore, on 22 February 1971, he assumed 'presidential powers' and on 12 March a plebiscite confirmed him as President for a seven-year term. Before that, Jadid had abolished the title of 'president' and replaced it with that of 'head of state', but Assad restored it.

The new constitution would be controversial, as in many places' protests erupted, especially in Hama, because it did not make Islam the state religion, although it stated that the President of Syria had to be a Muslim. The question then posed whether an 'Alawi could be legitimately called a Muslim. To solve this problem, Assad appealed to an influential Shi'i cleric, Imam Musa al-Sadr, head of the Higher Shi'i Council in Lebanon, who issued a *fatwa* or religious ruling that said that 'Alawis were indeed a community of Shi'i Islam. When the still unsatisfied opposition then rioted to demand that Islam be declared the state religion (something which had not featured in the constitutions of 1930, 1953 or 1964), Assad stood firm and secured massive endorsement for his secular constitution in a referendum on 12 March 1973.

Another development on which Assad set great store, and which had been a subject of dispute between him and Jadid, was the formation of a National Progressive Front in which political groupings other than the Ba'ath could also make a showing. The Front was inaugurated on 7

March 1972 after several months of haggling over the terms of its charter and the respective powers of the members. Besides the Ba'ath which necessarily dominated the Front, its other members were the Communist Party, the Arab Socialist Union (a Nasserist relic of UAR days), the Arab Socialist Movement and the Organization of Socialist Unionists. Later, after his son Bashar al-Assad took over in 2000, the Syrian Social Nationalist Party (SSNP) would also be allowed to join the Front and others like the Social Democratic Unionists.

Throughout Syria, something like a two-tier system was installed: at the base was the security bedrock of the regime and infrastructure of control in which 'Alawis were often but not exclusively to be found. Although

Assad was not a sectarian, he still
depended on his own community for
security and ultimate survival. On this
foundation, a second tier was erected
of administration, of economic
activity, of semi-representative
institutions, of public office and
private gain which could afford to be
more diverse and more open to all
the talents. During this time, threats
to Assad's rule still existed.
Muhammed Umran, the first leader
of the Military Committee had
started to plot against the new
regime from Lebanon, but on 4
March his ambitions were brought to
an abrupt end as he was murdered at
his home in Tripoli, Lebanon. Umran's
family did not blame Assad for the
murder and Umran's son, Najih called
on Assad some six months later and
wept in his arms.
Assad had longed to wipe away the

stain of defeat during the Six-Day War which had affected him personally and profoundly and to restore the confidence of his troops and recover the land and show the world that, given the chance, the Arabs could acquit themselves honourably. He was convinced that Israel had won the Six-Day War by ruse, catching the Arabs napping, but that it was not inherently unbeatable. He genuinely believed that the Arabs could snatch back and hold some if not all their lost land. During this time, he met many Arab leaders, including the new President of Egypt, Anwar Sadat. He also flew to Moscow to obtain the weapons required for the enterprise he had in mind.

Anwar Sadat, President of Egypt.

On 6th of October 1973, Egypt attacked across the Suez Canal in the south and Syria moved through the Golan Heights in the north. The early successes experienced by both sides in the war were primarily the result of deception and targeted military strategy. After initial setbacks, on October 8, an Israeli counteroffensive began on both fronts, but it stalled in the south against Egypt. According to Assad, the problem for him was that Sadat had never informed him that he entered the war with limited objectives in mind. Assad knew that he would not be able to fully defeat Israel, but he wanted to get the occupied Golan Heights back, a military objective he hoped Egypt shared with Sinai. Therefore, the Egyptian strategy enabled Israeli forces to concentrate to the north to stall the more immediate Syrian threat. This led the Soviets to begin a massive lift of arms and ammunition to Syria by October 10. Assad also had found out that Sadat had entered into secret talks with American Secretary of State Henry Kissinger at the beginning of the war. Because of this, Assad was furious and communications between Cairo and Damascus deteriorated. During this time, Israeli forces were only 20 miles from Damascus. Sadat finally relented and on 14 October launched an offensive. By October 15, Israel had launched its second counteroffensive, emboldened by the US airlift that had followed a day before. Syrian and Egyptian forces were now on the defensive. At this point, on October 19, the Arab members of OPEC launched an oil embargo. The Kremlin also began to threaten that it would intervene directly into the war. United States put its nuclear forces on its highest alert since the Cuban Missile Crisis and places pressure on Israel to negotiate a cease-fire via the United Nations, passing UN Security Council Resolution 337 on October 22. The war ended on October 25 and Israel would give back the newly occupied territories, although not the Golan Heights. Syria and Egypt had lost much more men and material than Israel, but Israel was bloodied and at least Syria and Egypt could claim a psychological victory. The oil embargo was lifted in March 1974.

Defence Minister Mustafa Tlass (in the middle) and President of Syria Hafez al-Assad (on the right) on the Golan Front.

Assad was not able to get the Golan Heights back to Syria. In 1974, Syria and Israel signed a ceasefire agreement. It established a demilitarized zone along their frontier. Israel also agreed to return about 5% of the territory to Syrian civilian control. This part was incorporated into the demilitarized zone and the strip was put under the control of the United Nations Disengagement Observer Force (UNDOF). In June 1974, President of the United States Richard Nixon visited many Middle Eastern Countries, one of them being Syria where he was greeted by Assad. Assad and his colleagues came to believe that Nixon was ready to commit the United States to search for a comprehensive settlement, but that Kissinger torpedoed the president's intentions, as Kissinger was as assiduous in helping Israel as he was in dividing the Arabs and believed like the Israeli Prime Minister Golda Meir that Golan Heights should not be given back to Syria and that the Palestinians should not figure in the invitations to

Geneva talks. Meanwhile, Assad and Nixon got well in their meeting and Nixon was impressed by Assad, however on August 8 under the threat of impeachment, Nixon resigned due to the Watergate Scandal and Gerald Ford who was not very experienced in foreign policy took over, which made Kissinger more powerful than ever.

Assad greeting Nixon at the Damascus Airport, 1974.

Assad (in the middle) talking to Nixon (on the left) while American Secretary of State Henry Kissinger (on the right) is listening, 1974.

Happy moments from the meeting, 1974.

Chapter 7 – The Peacemaker

In 1975, a civil war broke out in Lebanon. By the end of the year, the war had claimed thousands of lives. The warfare in Lebanon posed a threat to the security of Syria. At the heart of the problem lay the Palestinians. Over 150,000 of them had taken refuge in Lebanon after the 1948 war. By the mid-1970's it had grown to about 400,000. From December 1975, the development in Lebanon caused Assad extreme alarm. He envisioned two options, both horrendous for Syria. One would be that the Maronite Christians would form their own state, which would bring Israel as its protector and the second due to the new persecution the Maronites were facing Israel would decide to intervene to punish the Palestinians.

Assad tried to persuade the warring sides to agree on reforms, with no success. Assad decided to intervene militarily. On the night of 31 May to 1 June 1976, Syrian armoured columns crossed the border in strength and immediately broke the Palestinian and leftist siege on several Christian settlements, notably the important town of Zahlé in the Beqaa valley. The summer of 1976 was spent in low-level military operations alternating with renewed appeals and ultimatums. In September and October, Assad launched several major offensives which ended in the near rout of the Palestinians and their allies. Although he fought against the Palestinians and protected the Christians in order to deny Israel a pretext for intervention, it proved to be in vain. By the end of 1976, Israel was more deeply involved in

Lebanese affairs than ever. Therefore, for Syria the Christians were thankless, the Palestinians hostile and Israel now as much a part of the Lebanese scene as Syria itself. Assad had fallen into Lebanese quagmire.

When Democratic candidate Jimmy Carter defeated the Republican incumbent Gerald Ford in 1976 US Presidential Election, Assad sent the president-elect Carter a congratulatory telegram in which he called for 'a fair US attitude' towards the Arab-Israeli conflict and spelt out his peace terms. They included: Israeli withdrawal from Arab territories occupied in 1967 and the restoration of the 'legitimate rights' of the Palestinians. However, Assad, like the other Arab leaders did not grasp how radically Carter was proposing to depart from the assumptions and the procedures of the Kissinger era, and how much help he would need from the Arabs if he were to succeed. Assad met Carter at the Geneva Intercontinental on 9 May 1977. He was gratified to see an attentive Carter nodding and taking notes. Assad felt that Carter grasped the essence of the Arab-Israeli problem, an enormous step forward from his standpoint. The two men got on well. Carter disarmingly remarked that they were both country boys made good and they were soon at ease with each other. (Carter before joining politics was a peanut farmer). Carter saw Assad as a self-confident leader of an independent mind whose sense of the past endowed him with patience to confront the future and Assad was happy that Carter had an open mind on the two critical issues of Palestinian rights and Israeli withdrawal from the occupied territories.

Hafez al-Assad and Jimmy Carter.

However, for Assad, the good relations would not materialise in productive gain for Syria. In 1978 Camp David Accords were signed between Egypt and Israel. It shocked the rest of the Arab world. While Israel withdrew in stages from occupied Egyptian territory as envisaged under the treaty, Syria was left facing Israel across the demilitarised UN buffer zone on the Golan Heights without an ally. Israel took advantage of this to give its occupation of the Golan Heights an increasing air of permanence and formally annexed the area in 1981, which was a grotesque breach of international law. By that time, Ronald Reagan was the new American President. The US voted for the UN Security Council Resolution condemning the annexation, but Reagan took no further action and tolerated the behaviour of Israel.

Chapter 8 – The Fighter

During his first decade in power, Assad did not have many strong internal threats to his rule, but during the late 1970s and early 1980s they would come fast and they would come quick.

Despite being popular at first when taking over from Salah Jadid in 1969, by the late 1970s corruption in Syria began to increase and the Ba'athist Party was seen more and more as the symbol of corruption. A lucky few with access to the government were acquiring vast wealth. The ruling Ba'ath party, as well as the higher echelons of the military and the government, were packed with careerists and profiteers. One of the people in the regime who was becoming richer every year was

Assad's brother Rif'at whose also
became more powerful than he was
at the start of Assad's takeover.

In the late 1970s, assassinations
began to start. In Aleppo between
1979 and 1981 terrorists killed over
300 people, mainly Ba'athists and
'Alawis, but a dozen Islamic people
who had denounced the terrorists.
One of the worst outrages occurred
on 16 June 1979, when terrorists
slaughtered large numbers of 'Alawi
officer cadets in the dining-hall and
then let in the gunmen who opened
fire indiscriminately. Thirty-two
young men were killed outright
according to the official report and
another fifty-four wounded, but
other sources say the death toll was
as high as eighty-three. For the Ba'ath
regime, it was a declaration of war.
The terrorists responsible were

Assad's largest opposition – the
Muslim Brotherhood.

Assad hoping to steal the
opposition's clothes said that Syria
"will remain a proud citadel flying
high the flag of Islam! But the
enemies of Islam who traffic in
religion will be swept away!'. The
regime preached the use of 'armed
revolutionary violence' against the
'reactionary violence' of the guerillas
and it brought tens of thousands of
young men and women cheering to
the regime's feet. Assad himself
narrowly escaped death on 26 June
1980 at the hands of his Islamic
opponents. Terrorists threw two
grenades and fired machine-gun
bursts at him as he waited to
welcome an African visitor at the gate
of the Guest Palace. He kicked one
grade out of harms' way while a

guard threw himself on the other and was killed instantly. Assad's personal bodyguard, Khalid al-Husayn, thrust the president to the ground and shielded him with his body. A wave of fury swept through the 'Alawi community and with it a thirst for revenge.

The Islamic Front managed to carry the terrorist war to the capital, Damascus itself. In August 1981, eluding the security forces, the guerillas exploded a car bomb outside the prime minister's office and in September another outside air force headquarters and a third outside a Soviet expert's Centre in October. In their bloodiest operation on 29 November they killed and wounded hundreds of passers-by with a massive explosion in the Azbakya district of central Damascus where a complex of intelligence agencies was located. Assad was little seen in those days and when Anwar al-Sadat was killed on his fifty-first birthday on 6 October 1981, leaflets in Damascus threatened him with the same fate. The final battle between the regime and the Muslim Brotherhood would be waged in Hama.

Hama was a conservative city and had been a redoubtable opponent of the Ba'athist state. The ruin of the local nobles, the rise of the 'Alawis and the prolonged terror and counter-terror of the Islamic insurrection had brought the citadel of traditional landed power and Sunni puritanism to the end of its tether. On 2nd and 3rd of February 1982, the Muslim Brotherhood killed some 70 Ba'ath officers and the Islamic insurgents proclaimed Hama to be a 'liberated city'. In Damascus, there was panic, and the regime shook. This time every party worker, every paratrooper sent to Hama knew that this time the Islamic militancy had to be torn out of the city, whatever the cost. Behind the immediate contest lay the old-multi layered hostility between Islam and the Ba'ath, between Sunni and Alawi, between town and country.

The battle for Hama raged for three grim weeks. The first one was spent regaining the town while the other two hunting down the insurgents. The amount of lives lost is not fully known, with government sympathizers estimating a mere 3,000 and critics as many as 20,000 and more. Complicating an accurate count was the fact that many women and children fled through the cordon of troops ringing the city and were at first presumed to be among the casualties. Hama would be rebuilt on a massive scale as the old heavily damaged headquarters were bulldozed away and the whole of Hama was reshaped on a grand scale with ring roads and roundabouts serving entirely new quarters furnished with schools, clinics, playgrounds and shopping malls. The battle was won by the Ba'ath and the Muslim Brotherhood in Syria was crushed and the organization would never recover.

In 1979, the Islamic Revolution occurred in Iran overthrowing the Shah and establishing the Islamic Republic. Rather than denouncing the new regime, due to Assad's rage at the guerillas and at the Sunni establishment abroad who were sympathetic to the guerillas in Syria, Assad decided to reach out towards the new Iranian regime and cheered the Islamic Revolution. He sent the Ayatollah Khomeini a telegram of warm congratulations and a few weeks later sent him a gift of an illuminated Quran carried to Qum by Syria's information minister. The Ayatollah kissed the holy book and thanked Syria for the offer of asylum it had made him in October 1978, after he was expelled from Iraq and had not yet settled in France. The previous Shah regime was also pro-Israel, and this played a part of why Assad chose to back the new regime as it was committed to anti-Zionism and anti-imperialism. Assad before the revolution tried to persuade the Shah to press Washington to be more even-handed in the Arab-Israeli dispute, but nothing came out of it.

Syrian relations with Iraq also
deteriorated when on 29 July 1979,
the new President of Iraq, Saddam
Hussein announced the uncovering of
a plot against him hatched by some
of his closest colleagues – in the
league, as he alleged, with a 'foreign
side' soon identified as Syria. More
than fifty of the accused were
brought to a special court and a score
of them including some of the most
prominent men in Iraq were gunned
down by their party comrades,
Saddam Hussein himself to the fore.
Assad protested innocence and asked
Saddam for evidence of Syrian
complicity, which was not provided.
The most likely reason for Saddam's
coup was that before his takeover of
power, Syrian-Iraqi talks were held to
establish a Syrian-Iraqi federation,
which would have threatened
Saddam's power. However, after his

takeover of power, no federation would be established. When Iraq would invade Iran on 22 September 1980, starting the Iran-Iraq war, Assad would be one of Iran's supporters in the war.

In the 1980s, Assad faced many foreign policy issues, mainly from the Iraq-Iran conflict and the continuing conflict in Lebanon, where in 1982, Syrian assassins killed Bachir Gemayel, who was a pro-Israeli Lebanese President and Syria was accused of ordering the assassination. The problems would continue and would lead to the Israeli invasion of Southern Lebanon. However, Assad would face one more internal threat to his rule, which came from his brother Rif'at. On 12 November 1983, after working late in the ground floor office of his residence, Assad felt unwell. He went upstairs to bed, slept poorly and in the morning telephoned his doctor. After examining him, the doctor called in another physician for a second opinion. They recommended immediate treatment for a suspected heart complaint. Assad was taken to Al-Shami hospital in Damascus where he was placed in intensive care. He had long suffered from diabetes, aggravated by a sweet tooth, and as a young man had complained of headaches and eye strain. After he visited his brother in the hospital, Rif'at Assad had declared his candidacy for the office of the president. This did not end well for Rif'at as he did not receive support from Hafez al-Assad's inner circle and did not have enough support in the military. His loyalists later began the 'poster war' where Rif'ats posters were put up in Damascus, but the military, still loyal to Hafez al-Assad took them off and replaced with his. This poster war lasted for a week until Hafez al-Assad's health improved. Later, Rif'at ordered his loyalists to advance to Damascus, but the Special Forces Commander Ali Haydar refused to support him. Rif'at was removed from his positions of power and was named as one of the Vice Presidents. Later he was sent into exile and was later allowed to return for some time without a political role. All of his proteges were removed from power, thus Hafez al-Assad survived another threat to his rule.

Hafez al-Assad and Saddam Hussein.

Hafez al-Assad (right) with his brother Rif'at al-Assad (left).

Chapter 9 – The Elder Statesman

After he had dealt with the major challenges to his rule, from the mid-1980s Assad's rule became more stabilised and he did not face such large challenges as he did in the first half of his rule. The biggest problem he had to face was to choose a successor. At first, it was thought it would be Rif'at, but after their fallout, Hafez al-Assad's eldest son Basel al-Assad was chosen. However, in 1994 he died in a car accident and his second eldest son Bashar al-Assad was chosen to become his successor who was an ophthalmologist (eye doctor) in London at that time.

Basel al-Assad.

Bashar al-Assad.

The 1990s was a quieter decade for Hafez al-Assad than the previous two decades. During the Gulf War of 1990-1991, Assad supported the coalition to drive Saddam's Iraq out of Kuwait, which helped to improve Syrian relations with the Western powers. And like before he met many international leaders like American President Bill Clinton and Russian President Boris Yeltsin.

Hafez al-Assad and Soviet Leader Mikhail Gorbachev.

Hafez al-Assad and Supreme Leader of Iran Ali Khamenei.

Hafez al-Assad and US President Bill Clinton.

Al-Assad family

Nearly thirty years after his father's death in 1963, Hafez al-Assad's mother died in 1992. His brother Rif'at came back to Syria for the funeral. However their relationship did not improve as in 1998, Rif'at was removed as Vice President and in 1999, economic interests owned by Rif'at were closed by the government which sparked protests in Latakia by Rif'at's supporters which resulted in the destruction of all of Rif'at's remaining business interests in Syria.

In his later years, Hafez al-Assad's health weakened and he started to delegate more of his work to his subordinates. He died on 10 June 2000 after ruling Syria for nearly 30 years.

Hafez al-Assad left a large legacy. He built an infrastructure which has resulted in the Ba'ath party stably ruling Syria. His regime protected minorities and managed to keep a stable balance in the Alawite-Sunni divide in Syria most successfully compared to the previous regimes. He built friendships with Iran and Russia which his son Bashar would keep, and which would become the main supporters of the Syrian Ba'athist regime during the Syrian Civil War.

Printed in Dunstable, United Kingdom

72233130R00067